What's Your Name?

A guide to first names
and what they mean

By Beth Goodman and Nancy E. Krulik

SCHOLASTIC INC.

New York   Toronto   London   Auckland   Sydney

ISBN 0-590-43906-5

Copyright © 1991 by Scholastic Inc.
All rights reserved. Published by Scholastic Inc.

12 11 10 9 8 7 6 5   5 6/9

Printed in the U.S.A.   40

First Scholastic printing, April 1991

Contents

Where Do First Names Come From?

The Earliest Names

The oldest first names date back thousands of years. These early names were Hebrew names. Back in those times, people named their children in several ways. A child may have gotten his or her name because of the way he or she looked. For example, the Hebrew name Harim means "flat-nosed." The names of flowers, plants, and animals were also used for children. The name Deborah means "bee." Kids were named after places, too. Names of cities, towns, and sometimes even mountains were used as names for children. The name Afra was a popular boy's name taken from the city of Afra in Israel.

Names From Around the World

Through time names changed and more names were thought up. Each culture has its own methods of naming children. These methods have been passed on through the years. For instance, many members of the Ashanti tribe in Ghana, Africa, name their children for the day of the week on which they are born. If you are part of this tribe and you were born on a Monday, your name might be Swado, the Ashanti word for Monday!

Many cultures have used numbers and months for names, as well. The Romans were some of the first to do this. For example, the name Quintus is also the Roman word for five. Names that have been taken from months are still popular today. April and May are both common names.

Today's Names

Today, names can come from just about anywhere. Many names have been invented through letter scrambling. A scrambled name could be a name that is taken directly from another name but has its letters rearranged. For example, the letters of the name Theodora were scrambled to create the name Dorothea.

Other modern names have been made up by combining the first letters of a few words or by taking the first letters of a few different names and arranging them to form one name. The name Greyson can come from parents with the names Gregory and Sonia. The letters g, r, e, and y come from Gregory, and the s, o, and n come from Sonia. Another example would be the name Rickell, which is a combination of letters from the names Rick and Ellen.

In the past twenty to thirty years, the spelling of many first names has changed. Often parents change the spellings to give their children names that are a bit more unusual. A lot of times the letter i is used instead of a y. That's why Randy is often spelled Randi. Another popular way to change the spelling of a name is to drop the last letter if it's an h. That's how Sarah becomes Sara.

Boy Versus Girl

Not all first names are easily grouped into boys' names or girls' names. Many names can be used for both boys and girls. Some of the most popular of these names are Leslie, Tracy, and Jordan. But there are many others. Movie actor John Wayne's real name was Marion. Glenn Close is a movie actress. Michael Learned played the mother on the TV show *The Waltons*. Today especially, many parents are giving little girls names that were traditionally thought of as boys' names. Boy, oh boy!

Nick Is a Nickname!

Even though everyone has a legal name (that is, your real name chosen by your parents), sometimes a person is known by another name — a nickname. Nicknames can be affectionate, teasing, or sometimes even nasty. Many nicknames describe what a person looks or acts like. A person with bright red hair might be called "Red." Someone who moves very slowly might have the nickname "Snail." Lots of nicknames are just shortened forms of a person's name. Robert is often called Rob or Bob. Elizabeth may be called Liz or Beth.

Names are very important. You hear your name many times a day; you write your name all the time. A name makes you stand out in a crowd. But what really makes a name extra special is the person behind the name. You may find someone with the same name as you, but you'll *never* be able to find another person just like you!

Where Do Last Names Come From?

It may be hard to believe, but hundreds of years ago there was no such thing as last names. In fact, dozens of people who lived in the same village would have the same name. There would be Peter the fisherman, Peter the son of John, Peter with the black hair, Peter who was tall, and Peter who was short. After a while, that got pretty confusing, and sometime around 1400 people were given family names or surnames as we call them today.

Most American last names can be put into one of four categories: last names based on jobs, last names based on parents' first names, last names based on places, and last names based on descriptions of a person.

Working Names

The most common last name in the United States today is the English name Smith. That's because when last names were first being recorded in England, many people worked as smiths. A smith is someone who works with metals like iron or gold. Some last names are even more specific. A Blacksmith made horseshoes. A Silversmith worked with silver. A Goldsmith worked with gold. There are lots of other English last names that are based on people's jobs, like Miller, Baker, and Fisher.

The English weren't the only people who had last names based on their occupations. Ferraro is the Italian equivalent of Smith. In Chinese, the last name Fu means "teacher." The Jewish last name Cohen means "high priest" in Hebrew.

Names We Got From Parents

A simple way of giving someone a last name was to base the last name on the first name of the person's father. Mr. Johnson was John's son. Mr. Richardson was Richard's son. In Ireland and Scotland, the Mc, Mac, and Fitz in names Like McSorley, MacGregor, or Fitzhugh all mean "son of." In Italian, Giovani means son of John. In Spanish, Hernandez means son of Hernando.

Names From Places

Many last names came from the natural area around where the person lived. Hill is a popular English name. Mr. Hill lived on a hill. Mr. Rivers lived near a river. Since *del río* means "of the river" in Spanish, chances are Sr. DelRio lived on a riverbank.

Names that mean "mountain" can be found in many cultures. Berg means "mountain" in German, and DuMont means "of the mountain" in French. Some names come from other forms of nature. The Chinese name Lee comes from "pear tree." The Japanese last name Tanaka means "rice field."

Other last names are based on the name of the city or town where the family lived. Chances are Mr. Minsky came from the city of Minsk. Mr. Londoner probably came from London. Mr. Moskowitz was more than likely a citizen of Moscow.

Descriptive Names

If you go back in history and find the first man to have had the last name Gray, you will probably find that he had gray hair. Using physical descriptions to form a last name was a regular practice in most countries. In England, the first Mr. Longfellow was probably a tall man, and the original Mr. Armstrong was a strong man. In China, the first Mr. Chan was an old man, since Chan means "old." The German Mr. Klein must have been a small man, because Klein comes from the German word for "small."

Some last names were given based on the personality of the person. An English Mr. Merriman was no doubt a happy fellow, while a Mr. Moody had a less stable personality. In China, Mr. Wing's name was based on the word for "warm one," and the Czechoslovakian Mr. Pokorny's name was based on the Czech word for "meek" or "timid."

Other Ways of Getting Last Names

Several groups of Americans have not had their names handed down to them from generation to generation. Hundreds of years ago, few African people had last names. It wasn't until they were captured and brought to America as slaves that they were given last names. Those names were usually the names of their slave owners. Since so many slave families were split up and sold to different slave owners, many members of the same family often had different last names.

Some of the immigrants who came to the United States from Eastern Europe had their last names changed by the immigration officers who let them into the country. The immigration officers often changed names they found hard to spell or pronounce. Suddenly Mr. Rosenberg found himself Mr. Rose, and Mr. Goldfein discovered he was now Mr. Fine.

Despite the fact that not all last names have stayed the same from generation to generation, last names still give us a special look into the lives of people in our past.

The Top Ten!

Popular first names change with the times. Here are the ten most popular names in the United States by year.

Girls

1900

Mary, Margaret, Catherine, Elizabeth, Anne, Dorothy, Ruth, Helen, Rose, Frances

1930

Mary, Dorothy, Anne, Margaret, Catherine, Gloria, Helen, Teresa, Jean, Barbara

1950

Linda, Mary, Patricia, Susan, Deborah, Kathleen, Barbara, Nancy, Carol, Sharon

1980

Jennifer, Jessica, Melissa, Nicole, Stephanie, Christina, Tiffany, Michelle, Elizabeth, Lauren

1988

Jessica, Jennifer, Stephanie, Melissa, Nicole, Ashley, Tiffany, Amanda, Christina, Samantha

Boys

1900

John, William, Charles, George, Joseph, Edward, James, Lewis, Francis, Samuel

1930

John, William, Joseph, Richard, Edward, Robert, Thomas, James, George, Lewis

1950

Robert, James, Michael, John, David, William, Joseph, Thomas, Richard, Stephen

1980

Michael, Christopher, Jason, David, Brian, James, Robert, Matthew, Joseph, John

1988

Michael, Christopher, Jonathan, Daniel, Anthony, David, Joseph, Matthew, John, Andrew

Girls' Names and What They Mean

Girls' Names

Abigail, **Abby**, **Abbey** — Abigail comes from the Hebrew name Avigayil meaning "father's joy." Abigail Van Buren writes the famous "Dear Abby" advice column seen in many newspapers.

Ada — Ada is a German name that means "happy." It is also a Latin name that means "noble birth."

Agatha — Agatha is a Greek and Latin name. It means "good." Agatha Christie was a famous mystery writer.

Ah Kum — A Chinese name, Ah Kum means "like an orchid."

Aimee, **Amy** — This French name means "beloved."

Ainslee — Ainslee is a Scottish name that means "one's own meadow or land." This name is also used for boys.

Aisha — Aisha is an Arabic name that means "living."

Alice, **Ali**, **Allison** — These names originally come from Germany and mean "of noble birth." The name Alice became more popular after the book *Alice's Adventures in Wonderland* was published. Ali McGraw is a movie star.

Amadis — A Spanish name meaning "love of God."

Andrea — Andrea comes from a Greek word meaning "strong and courageous." Andrea McArdle is an actress who played Annie in the Broadway show.

Ann, **Anne** — The name Anne comes from the Hebrew name Hannah meaning "grace." Anne Frank was a Jewish girl who hid from the Nazis during World War II. Her diary, *The Diary of a Young Girl*, tells her story.

April — April is a Latin name. It means "to open."

Ariel, **Arielle** — This is a Hebrew name that means "lioness of God."

Audrey — Audrey is a German name that means "the noble one." Audrey Hepburn is an actress.

Girls' Names

Barbara — Barbara is a Greek name. It means "strange" or "foreign." Barbra Streisand is a singer and an actress. Barbara Bush is our nation's First Lady.

Basimah — Basimah is an Arabic name meaning "smiling."

Bena, Bina — Bena means "wise." It is a Hebrew name.

Bernadette — Performer Bernadette Peters is just one person with this French and German name. It means "bold as a bear."

Bernice — Bernice comes from the Greek name

Berenike, which means "a bringer of victory."

Beth — Beth is a Hebrew name and means "daughter of God" or "house of joy." Beth March, a character in the book *Little Women*, is a famous Beth.

Beverly — Beverly comes from Old English and means "a beaver's meadow." Beverly Sills is a famous opera singer.

Bianca — Bianca is an Italian name. It means "white."

Bliss — Bliss is an Anglo-Saxon name and it means "perfect joy."

Bo — A Chinese name, Bo means "precious."

Bonnie, **Bonny** — This name comes from a Latin word meaning "good."

Bree — Bree is a Middle English name meaning "a broth."

Bridget — Bridget is an Irish name. This name means "the mighty." Bridget Fonda, daughter of Peter Fonda and niece of Jane Fonda, is an actress on her own.

Brigitta — Brigitta is a Dutch form of Bridget and it means "strength."

Brilliant — This name comes from French and Italian words and means "sparkle" or "whirl."

Brooke — Brooke is an Old English name meaning "a dweller by the stream." A well-known Brooke is model Brooke Shields.

Girls' Names

Camille — Camille is a Latin name meaning "a virgin of unblemished character."

Candace, Candice — The name Candace comes from the Greek word for "fire-white" or "incandescent." Candace Cameron and Candice Bergen are two television actresses.

Carlota, Carlotta — Carlota means "petite and feminine." It's a Portugese name.

Carol — This French name means "to sing joyfully." Carol Burnett is a well-known comedienne and actress.

Caroline, **Carolyn** — Caroline comes from the English name Charles. It means "strong, virile."

Chelsea — Chelsea is an Anglo-Saxon name that means "a port of ships."

Cheryl — From a French word meaning "beloved."

Chitose — Chitose is a Japanese name. It means "thousand years."

Chloe — Chloe is a Greek name. This name means "blooming."

Chun — This is a Chinese name that means "spring."

Claire, **Clara** — These Latin names mean "clear and bright."

Clarissa — The name Clarissa comes from a Greek word meaning "grace, beauty, and kindness."

Colleen, **Kolleen** — This is an Irish name. It means "girl." Colleen Dewhurst is a famous actress.

Corah, Cora — Corah is an Indian name. It means "unchanging."

Crystal — A Greek name that means "a clear, brilliant glass." Crystal Gayle is a country singer.

Cybil — See Sybil.

Cynthia — Cynthia comes from a Greek word and means "the moon" or "the moon goddess."

Girls' Names

Dada — "Child born with curly hair" is what this Nigerian name means.

Dai — Dai is a Japanese name and it means "great."

Daisy — Daisy means "day's eye." It comes from Middle English.

Dana — Dana comes from the Latin word meaning "bright." It also comes from the Hebrew word meaning "to judge."

Daniele, Danielle — This is a feminine form of the Hebrew name Daniel. It means "God is my judge."

Daphne — This Greek name means "the laurel or bay tree."

Darleen, Darlene — "Dearly beloved" is what Darlene means. It is an Anglo-Saxon name.

Debora, Deborah, Debra, Debbie — Debora is a Hebrew name. The meaning of this name is "bee" or "to speak kind words." Debbie Reynolds is a movie star.

Denise — This name comes from the Greek god Dionysus, the god of wine.

Deolinda — This is a Portuguese name meaning "beautiful God."

Diana, **Diane** — Diana comes from a Latin word. It means "divine." Princess Diana is married to Prince Charles of England. Diana Ross is a well-known singer.

Donna — Donna is an Italian form of a Latin word meaning "lady."

Dorisa — This Hawaiian name means "from the sea."

Dorothy — From the Greek word *daron*, meaning "gift of God."

Dory — Dory is an English name. It means "golden-haired."

Dyani — Dyani is a Navaho name. Dyani means "a deer."

Girls' Names

Ebony — Ebony comes from a Greek word meaning "a hard, dark wood."

Eden — Eden comes from the Hebrew language. It means "a place of delight."

Edith — This is an English name meaning "rich and happy."

Elaine — This name is a French form of the name Helen. It means "light."

Eleanor — See Ellen.

Elizabeth — Elizabeth is a Hebrew name that means "God's oath." Queen Elizabeth II is the queen of England.

Ellama — This Indian name means "mother goddess."

Ellen, **Eleanor**, **Helen** — Ellen is a Scottish name that means "light."

Emily — This is the feminine form of the Latin name Aemilius. It means "ambitious and industrious." Emily Dickinson was an American poet.

Emma — Emma comes from the Greek name Erma and it means "the big one" or "grandmother." Emma Samms is an actress.

Erica, **Erika** — This is the feminine form of Eric. It means "honorable ruler."

Erin — Erin is a poetic name for Ireland. It is also the Irish word for "peace."

Esther — A Persian name, Esther means "star."

Ethel — Ethel is an Anglo-Saxon name meaning "noble."

Eve, **Eva** — Eve is a Hebrew name meaning "life."

Evelyn — Evelyn is a Hebrew name and it means "life." In Ireland it means "pleasant and agreeable."

Girls' Names

Faith — Faith comes from the Middle English name Feith and the Latin word *fidere* meaning "to trust." Faith Ford is a television actress who plays Corky Sherwood on *Murphy Brown*.

Fala — Fala is a North American Indian name meaning "crow."

Farrah — This Arabic name means "lover of donkeys." Farrah Fawcett is a popular television and motion-picture actress.

Fawn — Fawn comes from a Latin word meaning "small deer."

Faye — Faye is a Latin name. It means "a fairy."

Felicia — Felicia is a Scottish name. This name means "lucky."

Feodora — This is a Russian name and it means "gift of God."

Fernanda — This Portuguese name means "adventurous and brave."

Filippa — Filippa means "lover of horses." It's a Swedish name.

Florence — This is a Latin name. It means "flowering or blooming" or "fair child." Florence Henderson is an actress who played Carol Brady on *The Brady Bunch*. Florence Nightingale was an Englishwoman who is considered the founder of modern nursing.

Frances — This is an Old French name. It means "free." Judy Garland's real name was Frances Gumm.

Francesca — Francesca is an Italian name, which also means "free."

Frayda — Frayda is a Yiddish name. Frayda means "joy."

Fuyu — Fuyu is a Japanese name. It means "born in winter."

Girls' Names

Gabriella — This is a Hebrew name. It means "God is my strength."

Gail — Gail is an Irish and Scandinavian name. Gail means "lively."

Gay — Gay comes from the Middle English word *gai*. It means "gay, merry."

Genevia — Genevia comes from Old French and Latin. It means "juniper berry."

Georgia — This is the feminine form of George. It is a Greek name. Georgia means "farmer."

Geraldine — This is a German name. It comes from two words that mean "spear" and "hard." Geraldine Ferraro was the first woman candidate from a major party to run for vice-president in the United States.

Gilda — This Old English name means "gold" or "coated with gold." Gilda Radner was a comedienne who starred on *Saturday Night Live* and in movies such as *Haunted Honeymoon*.

Gillian — This is an English name meaning "youth."

Gin — A Japanese name, Gin means "silver."

Gladys — Gladys means "princess" or "ruler over a territory." Gladys is a Welsh name.

Gloria — This is a Latin name meaning "glory." Gloria Swanson was a film star.

Grace — Grace is a Latin name meaning "grace." Grace Kelly was an actress and then Princess of Monaco.

Gryta — Gryta is a Greek name. This name means "pearl."

Gwen — Gwen is a Celtic name that means "white."

Guri — This Indian name means "goddess of abundance."

Gutka — Gutka is a Polish name and it means "good."

Girls' Names

Hanna, **Hannah** — This Hebrew name means "gracious."

Harmony — Harmony is a Greek name and it means "a blending into the whole."

Haru — This Japanese name means "born in the spring."

Hasina — Hasina is an African name and it means "good."

Hayley — This Norse name means "hero." As a child, Hayley Mills starred in many movies such as *Pollyanna* and *The Parent Trap*.

Heather — From the Middle English word *haddyr*, this name means "a shrub, a plant." Heather Locklear is an actress.

Hedda — Hedda is a German name. It means "warfare."

Helen — See Ellen. Hellen Keller was famous for learning how to overcome her handicaps of being blind, deaf, and mute.

Hilary — This Latin name means "cheerful."

Hildegarde — Hildegarde means "battle protector." It is a German name.

Hinda — This is a German and Yiddish name. It means "deer."

Holly, **Hollie** — Holly comes from the Old English word *holegn*. It means "a type of shrub with red berries."

Hope — Hope means "trust, faith." Hope is an Old English name. It's used as both a first and last name.

Hortense — Hortense is a Latin name meaning "gardener."

Hyun — This Korean name means "wisdom."

Girls' Names

Ida — Ida means "a possession" and "protection." It is an Old English name.

Idalee — Idalee is an invented name. The names Ida and Lee were combined to make it.

Imma — Imma is a Hebrew name. It means "mother."

Imogene — "Image or likeness" is what this Latin name means. Imogene Coca is a comedienne who became popular in the early days of television.

Ina — This name means "mother" in Latin.

Inga — Inga means "hero's daughter." It's a Polish name.

Ingrid — Ingrid comes from the name "Ing," the Norwegian god of peace and the harvest. Ingrid Bergman was a famous movie actress.

Irene — Irene means "peace." It's a Greek name.

Iris — Iris is a Greek name and it means "rainbow."

Isabel, **Isabelle** — This name means "oath of God." It's a Hebrew name.

Isadora — Isadora comes from the Greek, meaning "gift of Isis." Isis was the Egyptian moon goddess. Isadora Duncan was a famous dancer.

Ituha — Ituha is a North American Indian name that means "strong and sturdy oak."

Iverna — This name comes from an Old English word that means "a bank or shore."

Ivy — Ivy comes from the Middle English word ivi. It means "a vine."

Iwalani — A Hawaiian name, Iwalani means "heavenly sea bird."

Izegbe — This Nigerian name means "long expected child."

Girls' Names

Jacqueline — Former first lady Jacqueline Kennedy Onassis is just one person with this French name. It means "one who follows after."

Jane, Jean, Joan — Jane means "God's gracious gift." It's a Hebrew name.

Janet — Janet's a Hebrew name that originally comes from the name Jane. It also means "God's gracious gift." Janet Jackson is an award-winning singer and dancer.

Jennifer — From the Celtic name, Guenevere, which means "the white or fair one."

Jennelle — This is an invented name that came from combining Jenny and Nell.

Jessica — Jessica is a Hebrew name that means "God's grace and riches." Jessica Lange and Jessica Tandy are well-known actresses.

Jill — This Old English name means "a sweetheart."

Jocelyn — A Latin name, Jocelyn means "just, fair, and honest."

Jordan — Jordan is a Hebrew name that is used for both boys and girls. It means "to flow down," or "descend."

Joyce — Joyce is an Old French and Latin name. It means "to delight" and "a jewel."

Judith — This name means "the praised" and is a Hebrew name that comes from the name Judah.

Julie — Julie is a Latin and Greek name. Julie means "belonging to the family or tribe of Julius." Julie Andrews is the singer and actress who played Mary Poppins in *Mary Poppins* and Maria in *The Sound of Music*.

June — June is a Latin name. The name comes from the goddess Juno and it means "queenly power." June Cunningham Croly was one of the first female newspaper reporters in the United States.

Justine — Justine means "justice" and is a Latin name. Justine Bateman is an actress.

Girls' Names

Kaimana — This is a Hawaiian name meaning "diamond."

Kali — Kali is an Indian name that means "energy."

Karen — Karen is a Greek and Danish name. This name means "pure." Karen Carpenter was a famous singer.

Karoly — A Hungarian name, Karoly means "song of joy."

Katherine, Katharine, Catherine — Katherine's a Greek name that also means "pure." Many queens and saints have been named Catherine. Katharine Hepburn is a famous actress.

Kay — Also a Greek name, Kay means "to rejoice."

Kelly — Kelly was originally an Irish last name meaning "warrior." Kelly green is a bright shade of green.

Kendra — This name is from Old English and means "head" or "children."

Keshet — Keshet is a Hebrew name and it means "rainbow."

Kimberly — Kimberly's a Celtic name. It means "the little valley or meadow."

Kirsten — This is an Old English name. Kirsten means "stone church."

Kismet — This Arabic name means "fate, destiny."

Kitra — Kitra is a Hebrew name. Kitra comes from the Hebrew word *keter*, which means "crown."

Kolleen — See Colleen.

Kohana — This Japanese name means "little flower."

Kyla — Kyla is a Greek name and it is a word for an ancient two-handled drinking cup.

Kyrene — This is another Greek name. Kyrene means "a lord."

Kunto — Kunto is an African name that means "third child."

Girls' Names

Laura, **Laurie**, **Lori** — This is a Latin name. This name means "laurel or bay tree." Laura Ingalls Wilder was an author who wrote the *Little House* books.

Lavena — Lavena is a Hungarian name that means "joy."

Leah — Leah is a Hebrew name and it means "the foresaken." Leah Thompson played Michael J. Fox's mother in the *Back to the Future* movies.

Lee, **Leigh** — Lee is a girl's and boy's name. It comes from Old English and means "meadow" or "sheltered." Lee is also used as a last name.

Leigh — See Lee.

Leila — This Arabic name means "dark, oriental beauty" or "night."

Leoti — Leoti is an American Indian name. It means "prairie flower."

Lesley, **Leslie** — This is a Scottish name that means "low meadow."

Leticia — A Latin name, Leticia means "gladness."

Liana — Liana is a French name and it means "to bind or wrap."

Lillian — Lillian is a Greek name and it means "a lily."

Linda — A Spanish name, Linda means "pretty or beautiful."

Lindsay — This is a German name. Lindsay is another name that's used for both boys and girls. It means "from the linden tree by the sea." Lindsay Wagner is a TV actress.

Lisa — Lisa is a Hebrew name. It means "oath of God."

Lisbeth — This German name means "consecrated to God."

Liv — A Norwegian name, Liv means "life."

Lixue — Lixue's a Chinese name and it means "beautiful snow."

Lori — See Laura.

Louisa, **Louise** — Louisa is a German name. "Famous warrier" is what this name means. Louisa May Alcott wrote the book *Little Women*.

Lucille — Lucille is a Latin name. Lucille means "light." Lucille Ball starred in TV's *I Love Lucy*.

Lulu — This African name means "pearl."

Lynn, **Lynne** — This name means "a waterfall or a pool." Lynn's an Irish name. Lynn can also be used as a last name as in Loretta Lynn, a country music singer.

Girls' Names

Marcia, **Marsha** — This is a Latin name. The name comes from the Roman god of war, Mars, and means "a warrior."

Margaret, **Peggy** — Margaret is both a Latin and a Greek name. It means "pearl."

Marianne, **Mary Ann** — This name comes from the Italian name Mariana. It means "of bitter grace."

Marie — Marie is both Hebrew and Latin. Marie means "bitterness." Marie Curie was a French scientist who won two Nobel prizes.

Marilyn — Marilyn is a Hebrew name. The name means a "bitter pool." Marilyn Monroe was a movie star in the 1950s and 1960s.

Marjorie — This is a Scottish name meaning "a child of moonlight."

Martha — Martha is an ancient Israeli name. It means "a lady." Martha Washington was the first First Lady of our country.

Mary — Mary is a Hebrew name. It's one of the most popular names and it means "a place of bitter waters."

Maureen — Maureen is an Irish name. Maureen comes from Mary and means "bitter." It also has another meaning in Ireland: "the dark one." Maureen O'Sullivan and Maureen O'Hara were two movie stars.

May — May is an Old English name meaning "a flower."

Melanie — This is a Greek name. It means "the dark" or "black." Melanie Griffith is the actress who starred in *Working Girl*.

Melinda — Melinda is a Greek name that means "gentle."

Melissa — Melissa is also Greek. It means "honey." Melissa Gilbert is a well-known actress who starred in the *Little House on the Prairie* television series.

Meredith — A Welsh name, Meredith means "protector of the sea." Meredith Baxter Birney is a television actress.

Meri — Meri is Hebrew. It means "rebellious."

Meryl, Muriel — This is an Irish name. It means "bright sea." Meryl Streep is an Academy Award-winning movie actress.

Mia — Mia is short for the Hebrew name Michaela. Mia means "who is like God." Mia Farrow is a movie actress.

Michelle — Michelle is Hebrew. This name means the same thing Michael does: "who is like unto the Lord."

Mildred — This Old English name means "mild strength."

Mindy — A German name, Mindy means "loving memory."

Misty — This Old English name means "covered with mist."

Moana — Moana is a Hawaiian name. Moana means "ocean, open sea."

Mona — Mona is an Irish name. Mona means "noble."

Monica, Monique — Monica means "an advisor." The origin of this name is unknown.

Moyna — Moyna means "soft." It is a Celtic name.

Muriel — See Meryl.

Myrna — This Greek and Arabic name means "sorrowful."

Myrtle — Myrtle means "tree or shrub." The name is Greek in origin.

Girls' Names

Naava — Naava is Hebrew. It means "beautiful, pleasant."

Nadia — Nadia means "hope." Nadia Comaneci is a former Olympic gymnast with this Slavic name.

Nadine — A French name also meaning "hope."

Nancy — Nancy is a Hebrew name meaning "gracious." Nancy Reagan was a First Lady of our country.

Naomi — Naomi is Hebrew. It means "beautiful, pleasant, delightful."

Nara — Nara is a Celtic name that means "happy."

Narkissa — This Russian name means "daffodil."

Natalia — Natalia is Portuguese and means "born at Christmas."

Natalie — Actress Natalie Wood was just one person with this French and German name that means "to be born."

Nedra — Nedra is a Middle English name and

means "below the surface of the earth."

Nerissa — This is a Greek name that means "sea snail."

Neva — Neva means "snow." Neva is a Spanish name.

Nicole — A Greek name, Nicole means "victory of the people."

Nina — Nina is a French name. It means "grace" or "granddaughter."

Nipa — Nipa means "stream." It is an Indian name.

Noelle — This is both a girl's and boy's name. Noelle is French and Latin and means "song of joy."

Nola — Nola is a Celtic name. Nola means "famous."

Noma — See Norma. Noma is the Hawaiian form of Norma.

Nona — An English name, Nona means "ninth."

Nora — Nora means "honor, respect." Writer Nora Ephron and comedienne Nora Dunn share this Irish name.

Norma, **Noma** — Norma is a Latin name. It comes from the name Norman. Norma means "pattern" or "example." Norma Jean was the real first name of actress Marilyn Monroe.

Nyla — Nyla is an Egyptian name and comes from Nila, who was an ancient Egyptian princess.

Girls' Names

Obelia — This Greek name means "a needle, a pointer."

Octavia — This name means "the eighth." Octavia is a Latin name

Ode — Ode is African. Ode means "born along the road."

Odeda — Odeda is a Hebrew name. Odeda means "strong, courageous."

Odele — A Greek name, Odele means "a melody."

Odessa — Odessa is Greek. It means "of the odyssey."

Ofra — Ofra is a Hebrew name and it means "a young goat."

Ola — An Old Norse name, Ola means "an ancestor."

Olga — Olga is Russian. Olga means "holy."

Olivia — Olivia comes from the Latin word meaning "olive," or "olive tree." Olivia Newton-John is a singer and actress.

Olympia — Olympia is Greek. The name means "of Olympus." Olympus was the mountain where the Greeks believed the gods lived. Olympia Dukakis is an Academy Award-winning actress.

Omega — Another Greek name, Omega means "great." It is also the last letter of the Greek alphabet.

Oneida — This name comes from the Iroquois tribal language and means "standing rock."

Oona — Oona means "one." It is an Irish name.

Ophelia — This Greek name means "to help."

Ora — Ora means "light." The name is Hebrew in origin.

Orabel — This name is both Latin and French. It means "golden beauty."

Oralee — Another Hebrew name, Oralee means "my light" or "I have light." Oralee Wachter is a children's book author.

Orenda — This North American Indian name means "magic power."

Oria, **Oriana** — This name is Latin. It means "Orient, the East."

Oriel — This name comes from the Old French and Latin. It means "gold."

Oriente — Oriente means "the direction of the sunrise." It is Latin.

Orlenda — This Russian name means "female eagle."

Orli — Orli is a Hebrew name. Orli means "light is mine."

Orlit — This Hebrew name means "light."

Orna — Orna means "let there be light." It is another Hebrew name.

Ornit — Ornit is Hebrew. Ornit means "a cedar tree."

Orseline — A Dutch name, Orseline means "bear."

Osayimwese — This Nigerian name means "God made me whole."

Osma — Osma means "hero." It is an Old English name.

Ottilia — This Swedish name means "lucky hero-ine."

Otylia — Otylia is a Polish name also meaning "lucky heroine."

Ova — Ova means "egg." It is a Latin name.

Girls' Names

Page, **Paige** — An Italian name, Page means "a boy attendant."

Paige — See Page.

Pallas — Pallas is a Greek name meaning "goddess."

Paloma — Paloma Picasso is a jewelry designer and the daughter of Pablo Picasso the artist. Her Spanish and Latin name means "dove."

Pamela — This name is Greek and English. It means "all honey." Pamela Sue Martin is a television actress who once played super sleuth Nancy Drew.

Pandora — Pandora is Greek. Pandora means "all, totally."

Pansy — This French name means "to think."

Patience — A Latin name, Patience means "to suffer."

Patricia — Patricia means "one of noble descent." It is a Latin name.

Paula — This is a Latin name and it means "small." Paula Abdul is a pop singer and dance choreographer.

Pauline — A Latin name, Pauline means "small, little."

Pearl — Pearl is Middle English. Pearl means "pearl." Pearl Bailey was a singer.

Peggy — See Margaret.

Penelope — This Greek name means "a weaver."

Perpetua — This is a Latin name and it means "everlasting."

Peta — Peta means "bread." The name is both Hebrew and Arabic.

Petra — This Greek name means "a rock."

Petula — Petula Clark is a singer with this Latin name meaning "patience."

Phila — A Greek name, Phila means "love."

Philantha — This is a Greek name, too, and means "lover of flowers."

Philyra — Philyra means "to love music." It is Greek in origin.

Phoebe — Phoebe is a Greek name. It means "bright, shining one." Phoebe Cates is a TV and movie actress.

Phyllis — A Greek name, Phyllis means "a leaf." Phyllis Diller is a comedienne.

Pia — Pia means "pious." Pia Zadora is a singer with this Latin name.

Placida — This is Latin name meaning "to please."

Plennie — Plennie means "full, complete." It's a Latin name.

Pomona — Pomona is a Latin name. It means "fruit." In Ancient Rome, Pomona was the goddess of fruit trees.

Poppy — A Latin name, Poppy is the name of a plant.

Pora, **Poria** — Pora means "fruitful." It is a Hebrew name.

Posala — A North American Indian name, Posala means "farewell to spring flower."

Prabha — This Indian name means "light."

Prima — Prima means "the best." It is a Latin name.

Primavera — This Latin name means "spring-time."

Primrose — Primrose is both Latin and French and it means "the first rose."

Priscilla — This is another Latin name and it means "ancient, old." Priscilla Presley is an actress who was once married to Elvis Presley.

Prudence — Prudence means "cautious." The name is Latin.

Prudwen — An Old French name, Prudwen means "excellent."

Pua — Pua means "a flower." This is a Hawaiian name.

Purisma — Purisma is South American and means "purest."

Pyrene — Pyrene is a Greek name that means "of the fire."

Girls' Names

Quanda — Quanda is an Old English name. This name means "queen" or "companion."

Qubilah — This Arabic name means "concord."

Queenie — Another Old English name, Queenie means "queen."

Quella — Quella means "to kill." It's an Old English name.

Quenby — This Old English name means "the queen's castle."

Querida — Querida is a Spanish name. Querida means "sweetheart" or "to ask, to inquire."

Quilla — A Middle English name, Quilla means "a quill."

Quinby — Quinby means "queen's estate." It is a Swedish name.

Quinta — This name is Latin and means "the fifth."

Girls' Names

Rachel — Rachel is a Hebrew name. This name means "a female sheep."

Radella — Radella means "counsel." It is a German name.

Raina — This Latin name means "to rule."

Raisa — Raisa is a Yiddish name. It means "a rose." Raisa Gorbachev is the wife of Soviet leader Mikhail Gorbachev.

Ramona — Ramona is an Old French name, which means "wise protection."

Rani — Rani means "my joy" and is a Hebrew name.

Rapa — This Hawaiian name means "moonbeam."

Raquel — Raquel is a Spanish form of Rachel. Raquel Welch is an actress.

Raya — This Hebrew name means "friend."

Rebecca — Rebecca is Hebrew and means "to tie, to bind."

Regina — This name means "to rule." Regina is a Latin name.

Renata — A Latin name, Renata means "to be born again."

Renée — Renée is a French form of Renata.

Rhea — This name is Greek. Rhea means "protector of cities" or "a poppy." Rhea Perlman is an actress who plays Carla on *Cheers*.

Rhoda — Rhoda is a Greek name. It means "a flower."

Rhonda — This Celtic name means "powerful river."

Ria — Ria means "a small river" and is a Spanish name.

Rimona — A Hebrew name, Rimona means "a pomegranate."

Rita — Rita comes from the Sanskrit and means "brave" or "honest." Rita Moreno is a Broadway singer and dancer.

Riva — Riva comes from Latin and Old French. The name means "coast, shore."

Rivka — This is the Hebrew form of Rebecca. See Rebecca.

Robin — Robin is German and means "bright fame." Robin Givens is an actress.

Rochelle — Rochelle means "a large stone." It comes from the Old French.

Rona — This Gaelic name means "a seal." Rona Barrett is a gossip columnist.

Roni — Roni is a Hebrew name. Roni means "my joy."

Rosabel — This Latin and French name means "beautiful rose."

Rosalind, **Rosalyn** — A Latin name, Rosalind means "beautiful rose." Rosalind Russell was an actress. Rosalyn Carter was First Lady of the United States from 1977 to 1981.

Rose — This is the English form of the Latin word *rosa*. Rose means "any type of rose" or "rosebush."

Roseanne — Roseanne is a name made up by combining Rose and Anne. Roseanne Barr is a comedienne and star of the TV show *Roseanne*.

Roxanne — This Persian name means "dawn, brilliant light.'

Ruby — Ruby means "red, reddish." The name is Latin.

Rula — Rula is Latin and Middle English. Rula means "ruler."

Ruth — A Hebrew name, Ruth means "a companion."

Ryung — Ryung is a Korean name meaning "brightness."

Girls' Names

Saba, Sabrina — This Hebrew name means "old, aged."

Sabra — Sabra means "thorny cactus." It is a Hebrew name.

Sabrina — See Saba.

Sadira — This is an Arabic name. It means "ostrich returning from water."

Sally — See Sara.

Samantha — An Aramaic name, Samantha means "the listener." Samantha Fox is a pop singer.

Sara, Sarah, Sally, Sarita — This Hebrew name means "princess, noble." Sally Field is an Academy Award-winning actress.

Sarita — See Sara.

Savanna — A Spanish name, Savanna means "a treeless plain."

Scarlet, Scarlett — Scarlet means "a deep red color." It is a Middle English name.

Selda — A Latin name, Selda means "rare, precious."

Selene — Selene is a Greek name. Selene means "moon."

Selima — Selima means "peace." Selima is an Arabic name.

Selma — This Celtic name means "fair." Selma is also a Greek name meaning "a ship."

Senalda — This Spanish name means "a sign."

Seraphina — Seraphina is Hebrew and means "to burn."

Serena — A Latin name, Serena means "peaceful."

Shaina — Shaina is a Yiddish name. Shaina means "beautiful."

Sharon — A Hebrew name, Sharon's meaning is "a flat area."

Sheila — Sheila is the Irish version of Cecilia and means "the dim-sighted."

Shelley, **Shelly** — See Sheila. Shelley Duvall is an actress.

Sherry — Sherry is Spanish or French and means "sherry" (a kind of wine).

Shirley — Shirley is an English name meaning "bright meadow."

Sybil, **Cybill** — A Greek name, Sybil means "wise." Cybill Shepherd is an actress and model.

Simone — Simone is a French form of the name Simon. It means "he heard."

Sloan, **Sloane** — This is a Celtic name that means "warrior."

Sofia — This is the Italian form of the name Sophia.

Solange — Solange is Italian. Solange means "a special gem."

Sonia, **Sonja**, **Sonya** — This name is a Russian form of Sophia.

Sophia — Sophia is English and German and means "wisdom" or "skill." A well-known Sophia is the actress Sophia Loren.

Stella — Stella is Latin. The name means "star."

Stephanie, **Stephenie** — A Greek name, this means "a crown."

Stockard — This is from Middle English and means "a stump of a tree." Stockard Channing is an actress.

Subira — An African name, Subira means "patience rewarded."

Susan — Susan is a Hebrew name. Susan means "a rose" or "a lily." Susan B. Anthony was someone who fought for women's rights in the 1800s.

Suzette — Suzette is the French form of Susan.

Suzuki — This is a Japanese name. This name means "bell tree."

Sylvia — A Latin name meaning "forest."

Girls' Names

Tabitha — This is both a Greek and Aramaic name and means "a gazelle."

Tal, Talia — This Hebrew name means "dew." Talia Shire is an actress.

Tamara — Another Hebrew name, Tamara means "a date-yielding palm tree."

Tammi, Tammy — Tammy means "a twin." It is a Hebrew and Aramaic name.

Tania, Tanya — A Russian name, this name means "the fairy queen."

Tara — A French name, Tara means "a measurement."

Tatum — Tatum means "a tenth." Tatum is an

Old English name. Tatum O'Neal is an actress.

Tawana — This is an American Indian name. The meaning is unknown.

Thelma — Thelma is a Greek name. It means "a nursing infant."

Theodosia — A Greek name, Theodosia means "divine gift."

Theresa, **Teresa** — Theresa means "to reap." The name is Greek.

Thomasina — This Hebrew name means "the twin."

Tiffany — A Latin name, Tiffany means "three." Tiffany is the name of a popular singer.

Tova, **Tovah** — Tovah means "good" in Hebrew. Tovah Feldshuh is an actress.

Tracey, **Tracy** — Tracy Gold is a television actress with this Anglo-Saxon name. Tracy means "brave." Tracy Austin is a tennis player.

Truc — Truc is a Vietnamese name that means "wish."

Tsuna — A Japanese name, Tsuna means "bond."

Tuesday — This is an Old English name. Tuesday means "Tiu's day." Tiu was the god of war and the sky in German mythology. Tuesday Weld is an actress.

Tyne — This British name means "a river." Tyne Daly is an actress who has won both Tony and Emmy awards.

Girls' Names

Ualani — A Hawaiian name, Ualani means "heavenly rain."

Ulema — Ulema means "to know." Ulema is an Arabic name.

Ulla — Ulla is a Middle English name. Ulla means "to fill."

Ulrica — This name means "ruler all over." It is German.

Una — A Latin name, Una means "the one."

Unity — Another Latin name, Unity means "one."

Urania — Urania means "heaven." It is Greek.

Urit — This Hebrew name means "light."

Ursula — This is a Latin name. Ursula means "she-bear." Ursula Andress is an actress.

Urte — Urte is a Latin name meaning "a stinging or spiny plant."

Usha — Usha means "sunrise time." Usha is an Indian name.

Ut — Ut is a Vietnamese name meaning "last."

Uta — This name means "mountain dweller." It is a Spanish name.

Girls' Names

Vaino — This British name means "high."

Valencia — Valencia is Latin. This name means "strong."

Valentine — Valentine means "healthy, strong." It is a Latin name.

Valeria, **Valerie**, **Valery** — Valeria comes from a Latin word that means "to be strong." Valerie Bertinelli and Valerie Harper are actresses.

Vana, **Vanna** — Vana means "high." Television personality Vanna White is one person with this name.

Vanessa — This Greek name means "butterfly."

Vera — Vera is a Latin name. It means "truth."

Verne — This Latin name means "green, spring-like."

Veronica — The name Veronica is Latin and means "true image."

Victoria — Victoria means "victorious." Victoria Principal is an actress who bears this Latin name.

Viola — Viola means "a violet" and comes from Middle English.

Virginia — Virginia is a Latin name. Virginia means "pure."

Vivian, **Vivien** — Another Latin name, Vivian means "alive." Vivien Leigh played Scarlett O'Hara in the movie *Gone With the Wind*.

Volante — This Italian name means "to fly."

Vrinda — This Indian name means "a woman in Hindu mythology."

Girls' Names

Wanda — This Middle English name means "forest."

Wendy — Wendy means "a wanderer." It is a German name.

Wenona, Winona — Wenona means "first-born daughter." It's a North American Indian name. Winona Ryder is an actress.

Wilhelmina — Wilhelmina is both English and Dutch in origin. It means "ruler."

Winifred — This Old English name means "friend of peace."

Girls' Names

Xanthe — This Greek name means "golden-yellow" or "golden-haired."

Xenia — This name means "hospitality." This is a Greek name.

Xylophila — Another Greek name, Xylophila means "lover of forests."

Girls' Names

Yafit — Yafit is a Hebrew name and it means "beautiful."

Yolanda — This is either an Old French or Latin name meaning "shy."

Yvette, **Yvonne** — These French names both mean "an archer." Yvonne DeCarlo played Lily Munster on *The Munsters* TV show.

Girls' Names

Zelda — Zelda comes from Old English and the name means "rare, precious."

Zesiro — Zesiro is an African name meaning "elder of twins."

Zita — This South American name means "little rose."

Zoe — Zoe means "life." This is a Greek name.

Zofia — Zofia means "wisdom." Zofia is a Polish name. See also Sophia.

Boys' Names and What They Mean

Boys' Names

Aaron — Aaron comes from the ancient Hebrew language and means "lofty or high mountain." The first high priest of Israel was named Aaron. Aaron Burr fought a duel with Alexander Hamilton.

Abdullah, **Abdul** — In Arabic, Abdullah means "servant of God."

Abraham — Abraham is a Hebrew name and means "father of many." Abraham Lincoln was the sixteenth president of the United States.

Adam — The name Adam comes from the Bible. Adam was the name of the Biblical first man. In Hebrew, Adam means "man of the red earth."

Adolph, **Adolfo** — In High German, Adolph means "wolf."

Akio — In Japanese, Akio means "bright boy."

Alan, **Allan**, **Allen** — Alan is a Celtic name meaning "harmony and peace." Astronaut Alan Shepard was one of the members of the Apollo moon missions.

Albert — In High German, Albert means "noble

and bright." Princes and dukes like to name their sons Albert. Albert Einstein was a mathematician and scientist who is considered one of the most intelligent men of modern times.

Alexander, **Alex** — In Ancient Greek, Alexander meant "protector of men." Alexander the Great was a warrior who conquered most of the ancient world.

Alfred — Alfred is an Old English name that means "wise council." Alfred Hitchcock, the director of movies such as *Psycho* and *Rear Window*, is widely considered to be the master of suspense films.

Allah, **Ali** — In Arabic Allah means God.

Alphonso, **Alonso** — In Old English Alphonso means "noble."

Alvin, **Alvan**, **Alwyn**, **Elvis** — Alvin comes from the Latin word for "white." Alvin Ailey was a famous dancer and choreographer. Elvis Presley was an early rock-and-roll music sensation. He was known as "The King."

Andre — Andre is a Spanish name that means "strong and manly." Andre Previn is the music director of the Los Angeles Philharmonic.

Angel — Angel is a Spanish name that means "messenger."

Anguo — Anguo comes from the Chinese word meaning "protector of the country."

Arnold — Arnold is a German name. It means "mighty as an eagle." Arnold Palmer is a winning golf pro.

Ari — Ari is a Hebrew name. It means "lion of God."

Arun — Arun means "sun" in Hindi.

Augustus, **Augusto**, **Gus** — In Latin, Augustus means "revered." Augustus Caesar was the grandson of Julius Caesar.

Boys' Names

Balin, **Bali** — Balin is an Indian name. It means "brave soldier."

Barakah — Barakah means "blessing" in Arabic.

Barnabas — A Latin name, Barnabas means "son of the prophecy."

Barnett, **Barney** — See Bernard.

Barry — Barry is a Welsh name. It means "marksman" or "spear." Barry Manilow is a popular singer of ballads.

Baruch — In Hebrew, Baruch means "blessed."

Basil — Basil means "kingly." It is a Greek name.

Bem — Bem is a Nigerian name. It means "peace."

Benjamin — Benjamin is another Hebrew name. It means "fortunate." Benjamin Franklin, the famed statesman and inventor, is one of the founding fathers of the United States of America, and a signer of the Declaration of Independence.

Beno — In Kenya, Beno means "one of a band."

Bernard, **Bernardo**, **Barnett**, **Barney** — Bernard comes from the German language and means "bear's heart." Bernard King is a winning basketball player.

Berto — Berto is the Spanish name for "one who is bright and distinguished."

Blaine — In Old English, Blaine meant "source of the river." Blaine Peterson is a quick-skating hockey player.

Bong — In Korean, Bong means "phoenix." The phoenix is a mythological bird that rises, alive, from its own ashes.

Booker — Booker is an Old English name. It means "beech tree." Booker T. Washington was a famous African-American educator.

Booth — Booth is a Norse name. It is a "temporary dwelling." Booth Tarkington was the author of several books including *Seventeen* and *Alice Adams*.

Bradley, **Brad** — Bradley means "broad meadow" in Old English.

Brett — In the Celtic language, Brett means "one who comes from Brittany, France."

Brian, **Bryan**, **Ryan** — Brian is the Irish name for "one who has strength and nobility." Bryan Adams is a rock musician. Brian Piccolo was a football player. The movie *Brian's Song* is about his life. Ryan White was a crusader for the rights of AIDS victims.

Brock — Brock is Gaelic for "badger."

Broderick — Broderick is the Irish combination of the names Brad and Richard. It means "rich, flat land."

Bruno — Bruno means "dark complexion." Bruno Walter was a musical conductor with this Germanic name.

Bruce — Bruce is a French name. It means "woods." Bruce Springsteen is a rock musician known for his hits "Born to Run" and "Born in the USA." His nickname is "The Boss."

Bud, **Budd**, **Buddy** — In Old English, Bud meant "beetle." Buddy Ebsen was the star of *The Beverly Hillbillies*. He was also the first choice for the actor to play the Tin Man in *The Wizard of Oz*. Unfortunately he was allergic to the makeup and had to turn the role over to Jack Haley.

Boys' Names

Cab — Cab is a French name that means "the driver cabin of a truck." Cab Calloway was a bandleader and singer during the 1930s, 1940s and 1950s.

Cal — Cal is the Hebrew name for "a faithful person."

Calvin — Calvin means "bald." It is a Latin name. Calvin Coolidge was the thirtieth president of the United States.

Carey, Cary — Carey is a Welsh name and it means "rocky island." Cary Grant was a movie star in the 1930s–1960s.

Carmel, **Carmelo**, **Carmine** — In Hebrew, Carmel means "vineyard."

Carlos — Carlos is a Spanish name for "one who is strong and manly." Carlos Santana is a rock guitarist who played at the Woodstock music festival.

Carter — Carter is the English name for a "cart driver."

Cassius — Cassius is a French name. It means "protective cover." Cassius Clay was boxer Muhammad Ali's name at birth.

Cecilio — Cecilio is Italian for "blind one."

Cesar — Cesar is a Spanish name that means "long-haired."

Cedric — Cedric is a Celtic name. It means "war chieftan."

Chad — Chad is a Celtic name. It means "warrior."

Chaim — In Hebrew, Chaim means "life."

Chander — In Hindi, Chander means "the moon."

Charles, **Carl**, **Karl**, **Carrol**, **Carroll** — In Old English, Charles means "manly." The Prince of Wales is Prince Charles. Charlie Chaplin, known as The Little Tramp, was a silent movie star.

Charlton — Charlton is a name that is French in origin. Charlton means "Charles' town." Charlton Heston is an actor who played Moses in *The Ten Commandments*.

Che — Che is a Spanish name that means "God will increase."

Chen — Chen is a Chinese name. It means "vast" or "great."

Chevy — Chevy is an Old English name meaning "the chase." Chevy Chase is the star of the *National Lampoon Vacation* films.

Chip, **Chipper** — The name Chip comes from the Algonquin Indians. It means "the chipping sparrow."

Christian, **Chris**, **Kris** — Christian is a Latin name. It means "a member of the Christian faith." Kris Kristofferson is a country and western singer.

Christopher, **Kit** — Christopher comes from the Greek word meaning "Christ bearer." Christopher Reeve is the actor who played Superman. Christopher "Kit" Carson was a famed frontiersman.

Clarence — Clarence is a Latin-based name. It means "clear and prominent." Saxophone player Clarence Clemmons played with Bruce Springsteen's E Street Band.

Clark, **Clarke** — In Old English, Clark meant "clergyman." Clark Gable is the movie actor who starred in *Gone With the Wind*. In the 1930s and 1940s he was known as the King of Hollywood.

Claude, **Claudell** — Claude is a French name. It means "lame."

Clifford — Clifford is an Old English name meaning "a crossing near a cliff."

Cody — The old Anglo-Saxon name Cody means "a cushion."

Colby — Colby means "a coal town" in Old English.

Conan — Conan was a popular Middle English name that meant "knowledgeable." Sir Arthur

Conan Doyle is the creator of the character Sherlock Holmes.

Conrad — This German name means "wise counselor."

Cory, **Corey** — Cory means "helmet." The name has a Latin root — *korys*. Corey Haim and Corey Feldman are two of today's hottest young movie actors.

Craig — Craig is a Scottish term for "one who lives on a steep hill."

Curtis, **Kurt** — Curtis is a Latin name. Curtis means "court." Kurt Russell is a movie actor who has starred in such films as *Overboard* and *Swing Shift*.

Boys' Names

Dale — The Old English name Dale means "a small valley."

Dallas — Dallas is another Old English name. It means "house in a small valley."

Dana — This Greek name means "bright or pure as day." Comedian Dana Carvey is one famous Dana.

Dandin — Dandin is a Hindu name that means "holy man."

Daniel — Daniel means "God is my judge." It is a Hebrew name. Daniel Boone was a well-known frontiersman.

Dante — The Italian name Dante means "long-lasting."

Darcy — Darcy means "of the Arsy" (Oise River). The Oise flows into the Seine in France.

Darryl, **Darrell**, **Darlin** — Darryl is a British name that means "a grove of oak trees." Darryl Strawberry is a home run-hitting baseball player.

David — The Hebrew name David means "beloved." In ancient times David was the king of Israel. Davy Crockett was known as the King of the Wild Frontier. David Bowie is a rock star.

Dean — Dean is an Old English name that means "from the valley." Dean Jones was the star of the Walt Disney *Herbie the Lovebug* movies.

Denis, **Dennis** — Dennis is the French form of the Greek name Dionysus. Dionysus is the Greek god of wine.

Deshi — Deshi means "man of virtue." The name is Chinese in origin.

Derek, **Dirk** — This Old High German name means "famous ruler."

Desmond, **Des**, **Desi** — This name has both French and Latin roots. Desmond means "the world." Desi Arnaz played Ricky Ricardo on *I Love Lucy*.

Dexter — This Latin name means "on the right."

Doh — Doh means "accomplishment." The name is Korean.

Domingo — In Spanish, Domingo means "Sunday." A child named Domingo means "one who was born on Sunday."

Dominic — Dominic means "belonging to God." It is a Latin name.

Donald — Donald is an Irish name. It means "brown stranger." Donald Sobol is the author of the *Encyclopedia Brown* mystery series.

Dong — Dong is another Korean name. It means "one."

Douglas — Douglas is a Celtic name meaning "dark blue." Douglas Fairbanks was a silent movie actor who was known for doing even the most dangerous stunts on his own.

Drake — The Latin name Drake means "dragon."

Boys' Names

Earl — Earl means "a nobleman" or "a count." The name is Middle English and is still used in

England today to describe a type of nobleman.

Edgar — This Anglo-Saxon name means "riches." Edgar Allan Poe was the author of scary tales such as "The Telltale Heart" and poems such as "The Raven."

Edward, **Ned** — Edward means "happy guardian." It is an Old English name.

Eldridge — Eldrige is an Old English name that means "old fortress."

Eli — Eli means "up high." It is a Hebrew name.

Elliot, **Elliott**, **Elijah** — Elliot is another Hebrew name. It means "the Lord is my God." Actor Elliott Gould played Trapper John in the movie M*A*S*H.

Elmer, **Elmo** — Elmer means "famous." The name is Old English.

Elroy — See Leroy.

Elvis — See Alvin.

Emmanuel, **Manuel** — This Spanish name means "God is with us." Emmanuel Lewis played Webster Long on the TV show *Webster*.

Emil, **Emilio** — This Spanish name means "to be hard-working." Emilio Estevez is a well-known actor, screenwriter, and director. He has starred in several films including *Repo Man*, *Young Guns*, and *St. Elmo's Fire*.

Emery, **Emory** — Emery means "working ruler." The name is German in origin.

Enrique — See Henry.

Enzo — Enzo is an Italian name that means "ruler of an estate."

Ernesto, **Ernest** — This is another Italian name. Ernesto means "serious." Ernest Hemingway was the author of *The Sun Also Rises* and other novels.

Errol — Errol means "to wander." It is Latin in origin. The swashbuckling actor Errol Flynn was a screen star in the 1930s and 1940s.

Estéban — This Spanish name means "crown."

Ethan — Ethan means "permanent." Ethan Allen was a hero of the American Revolutionary War.

Eugene, **Eugenio** — Eugene means "born lucky." Playwright Eugene O'Neill is one person with this Greek name.

Evan — See John.

Everett — Everett is a German name. It means "a wild boar." C. Everett Coop is a former surgeon general of the United States. He is famous for his campaign against smoking.

Ezra — Ezra is a Hebrew name that means "help and salvation."

Boys' Names

Fabio — Fabio means "bean grower." The name is Spanish.

Felipe — See Philip.

Felix — This is a Latin name. Felix means "happy" or "fortunate."

Fergus — This Irish name means "manly."

Fernando — Fernando means "adventurous." The name is Latin.

Fidel — Fidel means "faithful." Fidel Castro is the leader of Cuba.

Fletcher — Fletcher is an Old French name. Fletcher means "arrow."

Forrest — Forrest means "outdoors." It is a Latin name.

Francis, **Fran**, **Frank** — Francis means "a free man." The name is Latin. Frank Sinatra is a popular singer. Fran Tarkenton was a Super Bowl-winning football player.

Franklin — This Middle Latin name means "a

free man." Franklin Pierce and Franklin Roosevelt were both U.S. presidents.

Frederick, **Fred**, **Fritz** — Frederick is a German name and it means "peace." Fred Savage is an actor who plays Kevin Arnold on TV's *The Wonder Years*.

Boys' Names

Gabriel — Gabriel is a Hebrew name that means "God's strong man." In the Bible the Archangel Gabriel is often pictured blowing his trumpet.

Gamal — Gamal is Arabic for "a camel."

Gary — This German name means "spear carrier." Gary Cooper was a famous movie star. Gary Shandling is a popular comedian.

George, **Jorge**, **York** — George is a Greek name that means "worker of the earth." Baseball hero Babe Ruth's real name was George Herman Ruth.

Gerold, **Gerald**, **Jarell** — This German name means "mighty with a spear." Gerald Ford was the United States's thirty-eighth president.

Geraldo — Geraldo is the Spanish form of Gerold.

Giancarlo — An Italian name combining John and Charles. See John and Charles.

Gilbert, **Gil** — Gilbert is a German name that means "pledge." Gil Hodges is a baseball Hall of Famer.

Giles — Giles is Greek. It means "from the goatskin" or "to protect."

Glenn, **Glen** — Glenn is a Celtic name. It means "of the narrow valley." Glen Campbell is a country and western singer.

Gordon, **Gordan** — Gordan means "three-cornered hill." It is an Old English name. Gordie Howe is an All-Star hockey player.

Graham — This Anglo-Saxon name means "gray home." Graham Nash sang with the popular singing trio Crosby, Stills and Nash.

Gregory, **Greg** — This Greek name means "watchman."

Grover — Grover Cleveland was the twenty-second and twenty-fourth president of the United States. He was one person with this Old English name. It means "one who dwells among the trees."

Gus — See Augustus.

Guy — Guy can be Celtic, French, German, or Latin. Depending on the origin, it can mean "sensible," "guide," "warrior," or "life."

Boys' Names

Hakeem — Hakeem is an Arabic name meaning "ruler."

Hamilton — This French name means "from the mountain."

Harith — This North African name means "cultivator."

Harold, **Hal** — Harold is a German name that means "commander." Hal Linden played Barney Miller on TV.

Harvey — In High German, Harvey means "army

battle." Funnyman Harvey Korman is a famous Harvey.

Hasani — Hasani is a name from Kenya. In Swahili it means "handsome."

Hector — Hector is a Spanish name. It means "defender."

Henry, **Harry**, **Hank**, **Enrique** — This High German name means "ruler of the house." Henry Aaron is the all-time home run hitter in professional baseball.

Herbert, **Herbie**, **Bert** — Herbert is an Old English name. It means "bright, excellent army." Herbie Hancock is a popular musician.

Herman — Herman is a High German name. It means "soldier."

Hiroshi — Hiroshi is a Japanese name meaning "generous."

Ho — Ho is a Korean name meaning "goodness."

Hollis — Hollis means "from the holly tree." The name Hollis is Old English.

Horace — This Latin name means "keeper of the hours."

Hugh, **Hubert**, **Hugo** — This German name means "intelligent mind." Hugh Lofting wrote the Dr. *Doolittle* books.

Humphrey — Humphrey Bogart, better known as Bogie, was an actor with this English name. Bogie's first name means "supporter of the peace."

Boys' Names

Ian — See John.

Idi — Idi is Swahili. The name is given to a child born during the Idd festival.

Igor — Igor is a Russian name meaning "farmer." Igor Stravinsky was a famous composer.

Imad — Imad is an Arabic name meaning "support or pillar."

Immanuel — Immanuel is a Hebrew name. The name means "God is with us."

Ira — Ira is a Hebrew name meaning "watchful." In the Bible, Ira was a captain in King David's army.

Irvin, **Irving**, **Irwin** — This Gaelic name means "handsome and fair." Irving Berlin was a songwriter who wrote "God Bless America" and "White Christmas."

Isaac — This Hebrew name means "he will laugh."

Isas — Isas is a Japanese name. Isas means "worthy of merit."

Isadore — This Greek name means "gift of Isis." Isis was the Egyptian nature goddess.

Ivan, Yvan — Ivan is a Russian name that means "grace."

Boys' Names

Ja — Ja is Korean. It means "attraction or magnetism."

Jabari — This Swahili name means "one who is brave."

Jacob, Jack, Yaacov — Jacob is Hebrew in origin and means "held by the heel." Jackie Robinson was the first black baseball player in the major leagues. Jacob Grimm was one of the Brothers Grimm who wrote fairy tales.

James, Jimmy — James is the English form of the name Jacob. Jimmy Carter was president of the United States from 1977–1981. James Cagney was a famous movie star.

Jammal, Jamal — Jammal is Arabic. It means "camel." Actor Malcolm-Jamal Warner plays Theo on *The Cosby Show*.

Jared — Jared is a Hebrew name and it means "to go down."

Jarell — See Gerold.

Jason — Jason is both a Greek and a Latin name. Jason means "healer." Jason Bateman is a popular TV actor.

Jay — Jay is both French and Latin and comes from the word *gaius*, which is a bird in the crow family. Jay Leno is a comedian.

Jed — Jed is Arabic. It means "hand."

Jefferson — The English name Jefferson means "son of Jeffrey." Jefferson Davis was president of the confederate states during the U.S. Civil War.

Jeffrey, **Jeff**, **Geoffrey** — Jeffrey means "gift of peace." The name is both English and German.

Jeremiah, **Jeremy** — Jeremiah is a Hebrew name and it means "God will loosen" or "God will lift."

Jerome, **Jerry** — Jerome is a Greek name meaning "of holy name." Jerry Lewis is a comedian.

Jesse — Jesse comes from the Hebrew word *yishai*, meaning wealthy. Jesse Jackson is a civil rights leader and the first African-American man to run for president of the United States.

Jesus — From the Hebrew name *Yehoshua*, Jesus means "God will help." In the New Testament, Jesus was the founder of the Christian religion.

Jimmy — See James.

Jin — This Chinese name means "gold."

Jo — Jo means "God will increase." It is a Japanese name.

Joby — The French name Joby means "persecuted one."

Joel — Joel is a Hebrew name and it means "God is willing."

John, **Johann**, **Sean**, **Evan**, **Shane**, **Shawn**, **Ian** — John is also a Hebrew name. It means "God is gracious; God is merciful." John Fitzgerald Kennedy was the thirty-fifth president of the United States.

Jonah, **Jonas** — This Hebrew name means "dove." Dr. Jonas Salk discovered the vaccine for polio.

Jonathan — Yet another name that is Hebrew in origin, Jonathan means "God has given."

Jordan — Jordan comes from the Hebrew word *yarod*, which means "to flow down."

Jorge — Jorge is a Spanish form of George. See George.

Joseph, **Joe**, **Yosi** — Joseph comes from the Hebrew word *yosef*, which means "God will increase." Joe Piscopo is a comedian who got his start on *Saturday Night Live*.

Joshua — Joshua means "the Lord is my salvation." It is a Hebrew name. Joshua Lionel Cohen invented the toy electric train.

Julian — This Greek name means "soft-haired." Julian Lennon, son of the Beatles' John Lennon, is a singer in his own right.

Julio — Julio is the Spanish form of Julian.

Jun — Jun is a Chinese name. It means "truth."

Justin — Justin is a Latin name. It means "honesty" or "justice."

Boys' Names

Kahlil, **Kalil** — This Hebrew name means "crown" or "wreath."

Kamal — This Hindi name means "lotus."

Kamil — In Arabic, Kamil means "perfect."

Kareem — Kareem is an Arabic name. It means "exalted." Kareem Abdul-Jabbar was a great basketball player.

Karl — See Charles.

Keith — This Gaelic name means "from the wind." Keith Moon was the drummer for the rock band The Who. Keith Hernandez is a baseball player.

Kendal, **Kendrick** — This Celtic name means "ruler of the valley."

Kenneth — Kenneth comes from the Scottish word *caioreach* and means "handsome."

Kevin — This Celtic name means "kind, gentle,

and beloved." Actor Kevin Costner is one famous Kevin.

Kim — Kim comes from the Greek word *kymbe*, which means "boat."

Kip, **Kipling** — In Middle English, Kipling came from *kypre*, "a cured herring or salmon."

Kirk — This Old English name means "church." Actor Kirk Cameron became famous for his role as Michael Seaver on TV's *Growing Pains*.

Kit — See Christopher.

Kiyoshi — This Japanese name means "quiet."

Kris — See Christian.

Kurt — See Curtis.

Kwan — Kwan is a Korean name. It means "strong."

Kyle — Kyle is a Gaelic name. It means "a hill where the cattle graze."

Boys' Names

Lal — Lal is a Hindi name. It means "beloved."

Lamar — Lamar is both Latin and French, and it means "of the sea."

Lambert — Lambert means "brightness of the land." The name is both German and French.

Lance, Lancelot — Lance comes from the Latin word *lancea*. It means "light spear." In the tales of the Round Table, Lancelot was the bravest of all of King Arthur's knights.

Lane — This Old English name means "to move" or "to go."

Laurence, Lawrence, Lorne — Laurence is Latin in its origin. It means "wreath" or "crown." Lawrence Taylor, the football player, and Sir Laurence Olivier, the actor, are two famous celebrities with this name.

Lee — Lee means "field" or "meadow." Television actor Lee Majors is one famous person with this Anglo-Saxon name.

Leeland, Leland — Leeland is a combination of the Old English word *hleo* and the German word *lee*. It means a "shelter."

Leif — Leif is a Norse name. It means "beloved." Leif Ericsson was an early Scandinavian explorer.

Leo, Leon, Leonid, Lionel, Lev — This Latin name means "lion." The MGM lion, the symbol of the movie company, is named Leo. Leon Redbone is a musician.

Leroy, Elroy — Leroy is a French name. It means "the king." Leroy "Satchel" Paige was the oldest man to pitch in a major-league baseball game. He was fifty-nine years old when he accomplished this feat.

Lester — This Anglo-Saxon name means "the shining."

Levar — Levar Burton is an actor who bears this French name. It means "the bear."

Liang — The name Liang comes from China. Liang means "good" or "excellent."

Lionel — See Leo.

Lloyd — This Welsh name means "gray."

Logan — Logan is a Gaelic name. It means "from the hollow."

Lorenzo — Lorenzo Lamas is an actor who bears this Italian name. It means "crowned with laurel."

Lorne — See Laurence.

Louis, **Luis** — Louis is an Old German name. It means "famous in battle." Louis Armstrong was a famous jazz musician.

Lucas, **Lucian**, **Luke** — Lucas came from the Roman name Lucius, which means "light."

Luther — This German name means "famous fighter." Musician Luther Vandross is a famous Luther.

Lyndon — Lyndon comes from the old English word lind and means "flexible." Lyndon Baines Johnson was the thirty-sixth president of the United States.

Boys' Names

Malcolm — Malcolm is a Scottish name that means "servant of Saint Columbia." Malcolm X was an African-American leader with this name.

Malik — Malik is an Arabic name. It means "king."

Manuel — See Emmanuel.

Marc, **Mark**, **Mario**, **Marcus**, **Marco**, **Marcos** — Marcus comes from the Latin name for the god of war, Mars. It means "warlike."

Martin — Martin is a French form of the Latin name Marcus. It also means "warlike." Martin Luther King, Jr., the famed civil rights leader and a founder of the nonviolent protest movement in the United States, was one famous Martin.

Matthew — Actor Matthew Broderick is one famous actor with this Hebrew name. Matthew means "gift of God."

Maurice, **Morris** — Maurice comes from the Greek word *mauros* and means "the Moor." Maurice Starr created the pop group New Kids on the Block.

Max, **Maximilian** — Max comes from the Latin word *maximus*. It means "great."

Maynard — This French name means "a hand."

Melvin, **Mel** — Melvin is an Anglo-Saxon name. It means "mill worker." Mel Gibson, star of *Lethal Weapon* and *Lethal Weapon 2*, is one famous Mel.

Michael, **Miguel**, **Mike**, **Mickey**, **Mikhail**, **Misha**, **Mitchell** — Michael is a Hebrew name. It means "who is like God?" Mikhail Gorbachev is the President of the Soviet Union.

Milos — This Greek name means "peasant." Milos Forman is a film director.

Mohammed, **Muhammed** — Mohammed is an Arabic name. It means "praised."

Morton — Morton is an old English name. It means "the town near the sea."

Murray — Murray means "of the sea." The name is Welsh in origin.

Boys' Names

Nadim — This Arabic name means "friend."

Nasser — Nasser is a Muslim name. It means "victorious."

Nathan — Nathan is a Hebrew name. It means "I gave." Nathan Hale was a Revolutionary War hero who spied on the British for the Patriots.

Nathaniel — Nathaniel is another Hebrew name. It means "gift from God." Nathaniel Hawthorne, who wrote *The Scarlet Letter*, was an American author in the 1800s.

Neal, **Neil** — Neil Armstrong, the astronaut and first man on the moon, is one famous person with this Middle English name. His name means "champion."

Ned — See Edward.

Nelson, **Nils** — Nelson is a Middle English name. It means "son of Neal." Nelson Mandela is a civil rights leader in South Africa.

Nicholas — Nicholas comes from two Greek words, *nike*, which means victory, and *laos*, which means people. Nicholas means "victory of the people." Nicholas Cage is an actor.

Nils — See Nelson.

Noah — Noah is a Hebrew name. It means "rest." In the Bible, Noah built an ark which he, his family, and pairs of animals, floated in to survive a great flood.

Noel — This French name means "to be born." It also means "a child of Christmas."

Norman — Norman is an Anglo-Saxon name meaning "a man from the north."

Nuncio — Nuncio means "messenger." It is an Italian name.

Boys' Names

Ogden — Ogden is an Anglo-Saxon name. It means "from the oak valley." Ogden Nash was a writer.

Oliver — Oliver means "from the olive tree." It is both Latin and French. Oliver Stone is a movie director who won an Academy Award for his film *Platoon*.

Orion — This Greek name means "son of fire."

Orlando — This Old German name means "of the land."

Orville — Orville Wright, one of the inventors of the airplane, and popcorn maker Orville Redenbacher share this French name. It means "golden city."

Oscar — Oscar means "divine strength." It is an Anglo-Saxon name. Oscar Hammerstein was a writer of Broadway show songs.

Oswald, **Ozzie**, **Ozzy** — Oswald means "god of the forest." It is an Old English name.

Otis — Otis is a Greek name. It means "keen of hearing."

Otto — Otto means "wealthy." It is Old High German in origin.

Owen — This name means "young warrior." Owen is a Welsh name.

Ozzie — See Oswald.

Boys' Names

Pablo — See Paul.

Paco — Paco is an Italian name. It comes from the Italian word *pacco*, which means "to pack."

Palmer — Palmer is a Middle English name that

means "pilgrim who carried a palm leaf."

Parker — Parker is a Middle English name. It means "one who takes care of a park." Parker Stevenson is a popular TV actor.

Patrick, **Patricio**, **Pat** — Patrick is a Latin name. It means "person of noble descent." Patrick Henry, a patriot during the Revolutionary War, is famous for his "Give me liberty or give me death" speech. Patrick Ewing is a basketball star.

Paul, **Pablo** — Rock-and-roll legend Paul McCartney is just one person with this Latin and Greek name. It means "small."

Pedro — See Peter.

Perry — See Peter.

Peter, **Pedro**, **Perry**, **Pierre** — Peter comes from the Greek word *petra*. It means "stone." Pete Townshend is a rock-and-roll guitarist.

Philip, **Phillip**, **Phil**, **Felipe** — This Greek name means "loving." Phil Simms, the football player, and Prince Philip of England share this name.

Pierre — See Peter.

Placido — Opera singer Placido Domingo is one person with this Latin name. It means "calm."

Prescot, **Preston** — Prescot is an Anglo-Saxon name that means "priest's home."

Prime, **Primo** — Prime is a Latin name. It means "first."

Boys' Names

Quenton, **Quentin**, **Quincy**, **Quinn** — Quenton is a Latin name. It means "the fifth." Quincy Jones is a record producer.

Boys' Names

Rafi — Rafi is an Arabic name that means "exalted."

Ralph, **Raoul**, **Randolph** — Ralph is an Anglo-Saxon name. It means "brave advice."

Ramon — This Spanish name means "mighty protector."

Rashad — This Arabic name means "integrity of conduct."

Ray, **Reese**, **Rhett** — Ray comes from the Old English word *ree*. It means "stream."

Raymond — This Old French name means "wise protection." Raymond Burr plays Perry Mason on TV.

Reese — See Ray.

Reginald — Reginald means "wise elder." It is an Old German name. Reggie Jackson is a baseball player.

Reuben — This Hebrew name means "behold — a son!"

Rex, **Roy** — Rex is a Latin name. It means "king." Sir Rex Harrison and Rex Smith are both actors with this name. Roy Rogers was a singing cowboy.

Rhett — See Ray.

Richard, **Ricardo** — This French name means "powerful ruler." King Richard I of England was known as Richard the Lion-Hearted because he was so brave. Former Beatle Ringo Starr's real name is Richard Starkey.

Robert — Robert means "bright fame." It is an Old High German name. Robert E. Lee, the General of the Confederate Army, and actor Robert Redford share this name.

Rodney — Comedian Rodney Dangerfield bears this German name that means "famed."

Roger — Roger is a German name. It means "famous spear." Baseball player Roger Maris is one bearer of this name.

Roman — Roman comes from the Latin word ro-

manus. It means "a person from Rome." Roman
Gabriel is a former football player.

Ronald — This Hebrew name means "to sing."
Ronald Reagan was the fortieth president of the
United States.

Ross — This English name means "meadow."

Roy — See Rex.

Rufus — Rufus is a Latin name that means "red-
haired."

Russell — This name comes from the French
word *roux,* which means "red."

Ryan — See Brian.

Boys' Names

Salam — This Arabic name means "lamb."

Salvador — Salvador comes from the Latin word
salvare, which means "to be saved." Salvador Dali
was a painter.

Samson — This Hebrew name means "sun." In
the Bible, Samson lost his strength when Delilah
cut his hair.

Sancho — This Spanish name means "saint."

Sanford — Sanford means "a sandy river crossing." It is an Old English name.

Scott — Scott comes from *scoti*, an ancient Latin name for people from a certain area in Great Britain. Scott Carpenter was one of the early astronauts in our space program.

Sean — See John.

Sebastian — This Greek name means "revered."

Serge, **Sergei**, **Sergio** — Serge means "to serve." It is a French name.

Seth — This Hebrew name means "garment." In the Bible, Seth was Adam and Eve's third son.

Shalom, **Solomon** — This name comes from the Hebrew word for "peace." In the Bible, Solomon was king of ancient Israel.

Shane — See John.

Shawn — See John.

Sherlock — Sherlock means "enclosed area." This Old English name was given to the literary private eye Sherlock Holmes by Sir Arthur Conan Doyle, author of the Sherlock Holmes books.

Silas — Silas is both Aramaic and Hebrew. It means "to borrow."

Simon — This Greek name means "he heard."

Solomon — See Shalom.

Son — This Vietnamese name means "mountain."

Spencer — Spencer Tracy, the actor, had this Middle English name, which means "butler."

Stacey — Stacey means "firmly established." It is Latin in origin.

Stephen, **Steven, Stevie** — Stephen comes from the Greek word *stephanos*, which means "a crown." Stevie Wonder is a rock-and-roll songwriter and musician.

Steven, **Stevie** — See Stephen.

Stewart, **Stuart** — This Old English name means "keeper of the estate." Stewart Copeland was the drummer for the band The Police.

Sylvester — Actor Sylvester Stallone is one famous bearer of this Latin name. It means "forest."

Boys' Names

Tad — See Theodore.

Tahir — Tahir means "clean" or "pure." It is a North African name.

Tal — Tal is a Hebrew name. It means "dew."

Taylor — This Old English name means "one who is a tailor."

Ted — See Theodore.

Telly — TV's Kojak, Telly Savalas, has this Greek name that means "gift."

Thadeus, **Thaddeus** — See Theodore.

Theodore, **Tad**, **Ted**, **Thadeus**, **Thaddeus** — Theodore comes from the Greek word *Theos*, which means God, and the Greek word *doros*, which means gift. Theodore means "a gift from God." The teddy bear is named for U.S. president Theodore Roosevelt.

Thomas, **Tomás**, **Tomasso** — Thomas comes from the Hebrew and Aramic word *t'ome*. It means "twin." Thomas Alva Edison invented many things including the light bulb and the phonograph.

Thurman — This Norse name means "son of Thor." Thor was the god of thunder and war in Norse mythology. Baseball player Thurman Munson was one bearer of this name.

Timothy — Timothy means "to honor God." It is a Greek name. Timothy Hutton is an actor.

Tito — Tito is a Greek name. It means "of the giants." Tito Puente is a well-known musician.

Tobiah, **Tobias**, **Toby** — This Hebrew name means "to honor God."

Todd — Rock star Todd Rundgren is one person with this Old English name. It means "fox."

Tomás, **Tomasso** — See Thomas.

Tracey, **Tracy** — This name, which is popular with both girls and boys, is an Old French name. It means "path" or "road."

Travis — Travis means "crossroads." It is both Latin and French.

Trevor — Trevor is a Celtic name. It means "prudent."

Troy — Troy comes from the British word *wye*, which means "water."

Ty — Baseball Hall of Famer Ty Cobb had this British name, which means "house."

Tyrone — Tyrone comes from the Latin word *tiro* meaning a "young soldier." Tyrone Power was a film star.

Boys' Names

Udo — Udo is a Japanese name. An *udo* is a plant in the ginseng family.

Ulysses — Ulysses S. Grant, general of the Northern Army in the Civil War, and later president of the United States, had this Greek name. Ulysses was the name of a Greek war hero in the ancient Trojan War.

Uri — Uri means "my light." It is a Hebrew name.

Boys' Names

Val — Val is a French name. It means "strong."

Van — This Dutch name means "from a particular city."

Vaughan, **Vaughn** — Vaughan means "small." It is a Celtic name.

Vern — Vern comes from the British word *ver* meaning "an alder tree."

Vernon — Vernon means "spring." It is a Latin name.

Victor — Victor comes from the Latin word *vincere*, which means "victor" or "conqueror."

Vidal — Vidal Sassoon, the hairstylist, has this Latin name. It means "life."

Vladimir — Vladimir is a Slavic name meaning "world prince." Vladimir Horowitz was a brilliant concert pianist.

Boys' Names

Wade — Baseball player Wade Boggs' name means "to wade." Wade is an Old English name.

Wahid — Wahid is an Arabic name that means "single."

Waldo, **Walter** — Waldo comes from the Old English word *waeald*, which means "woods."

Wallace — This French name means "one who cleans and thickens cloth."

Walter — See Waldo.

Warren, **Werner** — Movie star Warren Beatty's first name is Middle English. It means "to preserve."

Washington — Washington means "water." It is an Old English name. Washington Irving was a famous American author who wrote *Rip Van Winkle* and *The Legend of Sleepy Hollow*.

Wayne — Wayne comes from the British word *waun*, which means "a meadow." Wayne Gretzky is a world-famous hockey player.

Wendel — Wendel means "valley." It is an Old English name.

Werner — See Warren.

Whitney — Whitney means "a small piece of land near the water." Whitney is an Old English name.

Wilfred — This Old English name means "wish" or "desire."

Wilhelm — See William.

William, **Wilhelm** — William Cosby (better known as Bill Cosby) is a famous comedian. His name is Old French and it means "protector."

Wilson — Wilson is an Old French name. It means "son of William."

Winston — Winston means "victory town." This Old English name was the first name of Sir Winston Churchill, prime minister of England during World War II.

Wolfgang — Wolfgang comes from the Old English and means "wolf path." Wolfgang Amadeus Mozart was a composer of classical music.

Woodrow — President Woodrow Wilson's first name means "wooded hedge." The name is Old English in origin.

Boys' Names

Xanthe — Xanthe comes from the Greek word *xanthos* meaning "yellow."
Xavier — This Arabic name means "bright."

Boys' Names

Yaacov — See Jacob.
Yasir — This Arabic name means "wealthy."
Yehuda — This Hebrew name means "praise."
York — See George.
Yosi — See Joseph.
Yvan — See Ivan.

Boys' Names

Zachariah, **Zachary** — Zachariah means "remembrance of the Lord." The name is Hebrew in origin.

Zeno — Zeno comes from the Greek word *sema* meaning "a sign."

Zubin — Conductor Zubin Mehta's first name means "to honor." Zubin is Hebrew in origin.